# The Presidents Of Iran

Leadership, politics and power in

the Islamic  Republic

## CHRISTOPHER L. KURTZ

# TABLE OF CONTENT

The presents of iran

# Chapter 1: Iran's Political System: The President's Office

Iran's political, religious, and cultural history have formed the presidency, making it a singular and intricate institution. The president is a crucial part of the political structure of the Islamic Republic, which was established in 1979 as a result of the Iranian Revolution. An outline of the President's duties, authority, and connection with other parts of government is given in this chapter, along with information about the President's constitutional protections.

## 1.1 The Constitutional Structure

A maximum of two terms of four years are allowed for the popular vote election of the President. The President needs to be a citizen of Iran, at least forty-five years old, and well-versed in Islamic law. The Islamic Republic of Afghanistan's Constitution.

Iran lists the President's responsibilities and authority, which consist of:

Chief of Staff of the Armed Forces; Commander-in-Chief of the Armed Forces; Appointing and dismissing Ministers; Signing

International Treaties and Agreements; Head of the Supreme National Security Council

## 1.2 Authority and Accountability

In addition to the Parliament (Majlis) and the Supreme Leader, the President possesses broad administrative authority. Important duties include:

- Presiding over the Council of Ministers - Supervising the Execution of Domestic Policies - Representing Iran in International Relations -

Adopting Laws (pending approval from the Supreme Leader)

- Giving reprieves and pardons

## 1.3 Connection to the Almighty Leader

The appointment and removal of the President are major political and religious responsibilities of the Supreme Leader or Wali-e-Faqih. The Supreme Leader, who has the last word on important political and religious affairs, must collaborate closely with the President.

## 1.4 Parliamentary Relationship (Majlis)

The Parliament, which has the authority to impeach and remove the President from office, is the President's ultimate accountability body. To enact laws and carry out policies, the President must collaborate with Parliament.

In conclusion, the presidency in Iran's political system is a complicated, multidimensional post with a wide range of duties. To effectively lead the nation, the President must manage the complex ties between the Supreme Leader, Parliament, and other organs of government. In the next chapters, we will go more into the topic of the President's position in Iran's political environment, which is introduced in this chapter.

# Chapter 2: Background History

The Islamic Republic of Iran was established after the Iranian Revolution

A turning point in contemporary Iranian history, the Iranian Revolution of 1979 saw the monarchy overthrown and the Islamic Republic established. This chapter offers a thorough analysis of the historical background that preceded the revolution, the major players and events that transpired, and the immediate aftermath, which included the creation of the new governmental system.

## 2.1 Overview: The Pahlavi Dynasty

From 1925 to 1979, the Pahlavi dynasty controlled Iran and was known for its authoritarian policies, corruption, and Westernisation. Iran's Shah, Mohammad Reza Pahlavi, imposed modernization programs while repressing political opposition and dissent.

## 2.2 Reasons for the Revolution

Several things contributed to the Iranian Revolution, such as:

- Poverty and economic disparity - Political persecution and violations of human rights

- Nepotism and corruption - Cultural alienation and Westernisation - Religious resistance to the secular policies of the Shah

## 2.3 Notable Ads and Occurrences

- Ayatollah Ruhollah Khomeini: Well-known cleric and opposition figure who led the Islamic Republic's revolution and eventually rose to the post of Supreme Leader.
- Mohammad Mosaddegh: A nationalist prime minister who was deposed in a 1953 coup supported by the CIA, sparking public unrest.
- The White Revolution: The Shah's modernization initiative, perceived as an assault

on religious authority and traditional values,
intended to make Iran a modern, secular nation.
- The 1979 Revolution: An array of
demonstrations, work stoppages, and protests
that finally resulted in Khomeini's return from
exile and the Shah's removal.

## 2.4 The Temporary Administration and the Ballot

- Mehdi Bazargan led the Provisional
Government, which was founded in February
1979 but had difficulty holding onto power.

- 98% of voters in a countrywide referendum held in April 1979 endorsed the creation of the Islamic Republic.

## 2.5 The Islamic Republic's Foundation and the Constitution

- In December 1979, a nationwide referendum adopted the 1979 draft of the Islamic Republic of Iran's constitution.
- The President, the Parliament (Majlis), and the office of the Supreme Leader were among the institutions of the new political system that were formed under the Constitution.

In summary, a variety of political, religious, and economic reasons combined to propel the Iranian Revolution, making it a complicated and diverse event. Iranian history underwent a dramatic shift with the founding of the Islamic Republic, which would influence the nation's political, social, and cultural environment for many years to come. Understanding the historical background, important personalities, and occasions that culminated in the revolution and the creation of the new political system is crucial for comprehending the next chapters. This chapter offers a thorough explanation of these topics.

# Section 2: Iran's Presidents

Chapter 3: 1980–1981 Abolhassan Banisadr

- Early life and schooling - Political career before taking office - 1980–1981 Presidency - Removal and banishment

Chapter 4: Rajai, Muhammad-Ali (1981)

- Childhood and schooling
- Political career before taking office - 1981 president - Assassination

Aleksandr Khamenei (1981–1989) in Chapter 5

- Early upbringing and schooling - Political career before taking office - President (1981–1989)
Ascend to the position of Supreme Leader

## Chapter 6: Rafsanjani, Akbar Hashemi (1989-1997)

- Early life and schooling - Political career before becoming office - 1989–1997 president - Political and economic reforms

Mohammad Khatami (1997-2005) in Chapter 7.

- Childhood and schooling
- Political background before serving as president - President (1997–2005)
- The reform movement and its obstacles

Chapter 8: From 2005 until 2013, Mahmoud Ahmadinejad

- Upbringing and schooling - Political career before taking office - Presidency (2005–2013) Disputations and altercations

Chapter 9: 2013–2021 Hassan Rouhani

- Childhood and schooling
- Political background before taking office - President (2013–2021)
- The nuclear agreement and economic growth

Chapter 10: From 2021 to Now, Ebrahim Raisi

- Childhood and schooling
- Political career before taking office - Current presidency (2021–2021)

- Present issues and regulations

# Chapter 3: 1980–1981
# Abolhassan Banisadr

Iran's first president, Abolhassan Banisadr, was in office from 1980 to 1981. Born in 1933 in Hamadan, Iran, he attended the University of Tehran to study economics and law. Before becoming president, Banisadr was a well-known participant in the Iranian Revolution, acting as Ayatollah Khomeini's spokesman and being an important member of the revolutionary council.

Administration (1980–1981):

In 1980, Banisadr won a landslide win to become Iran's first president. Several significant occasions and difficulties characterized his presidency, including:

- Dealing with the Iran-Iraq War; - Putting the new constitution and political system into effect; - Managing the economy and foreign affairs; - Dealing with resistance from political rivals and clerical hardliners

Demotion and Banishment:

Banisadr's term as president ended. The parliament impeached Banisadr in 1981 on grounds of political instability and incompetence, ending his administration. Mohammad-Ali Rajai took his post, and he later escaped to France, where he is now living in exile.

History:

Although Banisadr had many difficulties and scandals during his administration, he is also recognized for his contributions to the development of the new political order and his advocacy of democratic principles. The political disagreements and ideological controversies of the day are reflected in his complicated and contentious legacy.

Important Phrases:

- "The revolution is not just about changing the government, it's about changing the whole system." "I am a revolutionary, not a politician," said Abolhassan Banisadr. "Abolhassan Banisadr"

Important Dates:

- Born in Hamadan, Iran, in March 1933
- President elected in 1980
- Removed from office: 1981
1981: fled into exile

Note: More information and commentary on Banisadr's life, presidency, and legacy will be added to this chapter, along with more quotes and dates.

# Chapter 4: Rajai, Muhammad-Ali (1981)

Iran's second president, Muhammad-Ali Rajai, held office from 1981 until his murder later that year. He attended the University of Tehran to study engineering after being born in Qazvin, Iran, in 1938. Before becoming president, Rajai played a significant role in the Iranian Revolution as the minister of education and a member of the revolutionary council.

President (1981):

Several significant occasions and difficulties occurred during Rajai's administration, including:

- Preserving the conflict between Iran and Iraq - Adopting Islamic laws and regulations
- Handling political dissent and disturbances - Overseeing the foreign policy and economic affairs

Assassination:

On August 30, 1981, an explosion at the Tehran prime minister's office resulted in Rajai's death. The political opposition group known as the People's Mujahedin of Iran (MEK) was responsible for the attack.

History:

Although Rajai had many difficulties and scandals during his administration, he is also credited with advancing revolutionary ideals and enacting Islamic laws. The political disagreements and ideological controversies of the day are reflected in his complicated and contentious legacy.

Important Phrases:

- "The revolution is not just about changing the government, it's about changing the whole system." - Ali Rajai and Muhammad
- "We will not compromise with the enemies of the revolution." - Ali Rajai and Muhammad

Important Dates:

- Born in Qazvin, Iran, in 1938

- President elected in 1981

- August 30, 1981: Killing

Note: More information and commentary on Rajai's life, presidency, and legacy will be added to this chapter, along with more quotations and dates.

# Aleksandr Khamenei (1981–1989) in Chapter 5

Iran's third president, Ali Khamenei, in office from 1981 until 1989. He was raised in Mashhad, Iran, in 1939, and attended Qom and

Najaf to study Islamic law and religion. Khamenei was a well-known religious and political leader who was instrumental in the Iranian Revolution before becoming president.

President from 1981 to 1989:

Throughout his administration, Khamenei faced several noteworthy obstacles and incidents, such as:

Establishing the Islamic Republic, consolidating power, managing the Iran-Iraq War, enacting political and economic reforms, and repressing dissent and political opposition

Ascend to the position of Supreme Leader:

Khamenei assumed the role of Iran's Supreme Leader in 1989 and continues to do so to this day. He has continued to exercise strong political and religious power in his capacity as Supreme Leader, influencing both Iran's internal and external affairs.

History:

Although controversy and political persecution have characterized Khamenei's presidency and leadership, he is also recognized for having preserved political stability and advanced Iran's economic growth. The political disagreements and ideological controversies of the day are reflected in his complicated and contentious legacy.

Important Phrases:

- "The Islamic Republic is a divine blessing, and we must protect it." - Khamenei Ali
- "The Supreme Leader is the guardian of the revolution and the Islamic Republic." - Khamenei Ali

Important Dates:

- Born in Mashhad, Iran, in July 1939
- President elected in 1981
- In 1989, became the Supreme Leader

Note: More information and commentary about Khamenei's biography, presidency, and leadership will be added to this chapter, along with more quotes and dates.

# Chapter 6: Hashemi Rafsanjani, Ali Akbar

- Born: Bahreman, Imperial State of Persia (now Iran), August 25, 1934

- Perished: January 8, 2017, in Tajrish, Shemiranat County, Iran, at the age of 82.

- Political Party: Construction Party executives Effat Marashi, who wed in 1958, is the spouse.

- Youngsters: Yasser, Mehdi, Mohsen, Faezeh, and Fatemeh

Ruhollah Khomeini's mausoleum is his resting place. He had two other political affiliations: the Combatant Clergy Association (1987–1996) and the Islamic Republican Party (1979–1987).

- Allegiance: Iran

From 1989 to 1997, Rafsanjani, a well-known Iranian politician and theologian, led Iran as its fourth president. He had a major influence on the political and social climate of Iran and was a pivotal player in the Iranian Revolution. He carried out several changes and programs during his administration with the goals of fostering economic expansion, strengthening ties with other countries, and loosening social restrictions. Rafsanjani made accomplishments, but his reputation is also tarnished by debates and criticisms, especially in light of his part in human rights violations and his role in stifling political opposition.

# Mohammad Khatami (1997-2005) in Chapter 7.

Iran's fifth president, Muhammad Khatami, was in office from 1997 until 2005. He was born in Ardakan, Iran's Yazd Province, in 1943. Khatami served as a parliamentarian, a priest, and the minister of culture and Islamic guidance before to becoming president.

President from 1997 to 2005:

During Khatami's administration, several noteworthy occasions and projects occurred, such as:

- Reform movement: The promotion of democracy, human rights, and the rule of law was the hallmark of Khatami's administration. The idea of a "Dialogue Among Civilizations" was presented by Khatami to foster mutual understanding and collaboration among nations.
- Freedom of the press: Khatami's administration loosened press regulations, which resulted in a growth in the number of new publications and a rise in the right to free speech.
- Women's rights: The administration of Khatami launched several programs to advance women's rights, one of which was the creation of a ministry for women.

Obstacles and Legacy:

Significant obstacles faced Khatami throughout her reign, including resistance from conservative political groupings and clergy. Khatami left a complicated and contentious legacy, but his reform movement eventually failed to accomplish its objectives despite his best efforts.

Important Phrases:

"The extremist era is finished." We must go into a discussion and understanding period." - Khatami, Muhammad
- "The most important issue is to establish a democratic system based on the will of the people." - Khatami, Muhammad

Important Dates:

- Born: in Ardakan, Yazd Province, Iran, in September 1943
- President elected in 1997
- Reelected in 2001 - Presidential term ended in 2005

# Chapter 8: From 2005 until 2013, Mahmoud Ahmadinejad

Iran's sixth president, Mahmoud Ahmadinejad, held office from 2005 until 2013. In 1956, he was born in Iran's Semnan Province in Garmsar. Ahmadinejad served as Tehran's mayor, a member of the Iranian parliament, and a regional governor before becoming president.

President from 2005 until 2013:

Throughout his administration, Ahmadinejad oversaw several noteworthy initiatives and events, such as:

- Nuclear program: Iran's nuclear program was advanced during Ahmadinejad's administration, which raised international tensions and sanctions.
- Economic policies: A cash distribution program and a cut in gasoline subsidies were only two of the populist initiatives carried out by Ahmadinejad's regime.
- Human rights: Ahmadinejad's government came under fire for its record on protecting human rights, which included suppressing political dissent and mistreating minorities and women.

International relations:

Ahmadinejad's administration took a combative stance in international relations, which included a divisive speech at the UN and a run-in with the International Atomic Energy Agency. International relations: Ahmadinejad's administration took a combative stance in international relations, which included a divisive speech at the UN and a run-in with the International Atomic Energy Agency.

Obstacles and Legacy:

Significant obstacles faced Ahmadinejad throughout his administration, including political opposition, economic hardships, and international sanctions. Many see him as an advocate of Iranian nationalism, but others condemn his economic mishandling and authoritarian inclinations, making his legacy nuanced and contentious.

Important Phrases:

- "The Holocaust is a myth." - Ahmadinejad Mahmoud
- "We will not retreat one step from our nuclear rights." - Ahmadinejad Mahmoud

Important Dates:

- Born in Garmsar, Semnan Province, Iran, in October 1956 - Elected President in 2005 - Reelected in 2009
The President's term ends in 2013

# Chapter 9: 2013–2021 Hassan Rouhani

Iran's seventh president, Hassan Rouhani, in office from 2013 till 2021. 1948 saw his birth at Sorkheh, in Iran's Semnan Province. Before becoming president, Rouhani served as a parliamentarian, a priest, and a negotiator for Iran's nuclear program.

Head of State (2013–2021):

During his administration, Rouhani carried out several noteworthy projects and events, such as:

- Nuclear agreement: In collaboration with the US, the EU, and other global powers, Rouhani's administration negotiated the Joint Comprehensive Plan of Action (JCPOA).
- Economic changes: Several economic reforms were carried out under Rouhani's administration, including a privatization initiative and a cutback in fuel subsidies.
- Human rights: Rouhani's administration came under fire for its record on protecting human rights, which included suppressing political dissent and treating minorities and women.
- International relations: Rouhani's administration took a more moderate stance in this area, making history by calling US President Barack Obama and traveling to Europe.

Obstacles and Legacy:

Significant obstacles to Rouhani's administration were political opposition, economic hardships, and foreign sanctions. His legacy is nuanced and contentious; although some see him as an advocate for Iranian moderation, others condemn him for not doing enough to protect political liberties and human rights.

Important Phrases:

- "The nuclear issue is a threat to our national security." - Hassan Rouhani "We will not abandon our nuclear rights, but we will also not pursue nuclear weapons." - Rouhani, Hassan

Important Dates:

- Born in Sorkheh, Semnan Province, Iran, in November 1948 - Elected President in 2013 - Reelected in 2017

- Presidency ends in 2021

# Chapter 10: From 2021 to Now, Ebrahim Raisi

Since 2021, Ebrahim Raisi has held the office of President of Iran. He was born in 1960 in the Iranian province of Razavi Khorasan, Mashhad. Raisi served as Iran's Chief Justice, a judge, and a priest before to becoming president.

2021–present: the presidency

Several noteworthy occurrences and projects have defined raisins presidency, including:

- Economic crisis: High inflation and a currency crisis are only two of the many financial difficulties Raisi's administration has had to deal with.
- COVID-19 pandemic: Raisi's government has put in place lockdowns and immunization campaigns to battle the pandemic.
- Foreign policy: Raisi's administration has persisted in pursuing an assertive foreign policy that emphasizes regional concerns and maintains tight ties with the US.
- Human rights: The human rights record of Raisi's government has drawn criticism.record, encompassing the handling of women and

minorities as well as the repression of political opposition.

Obstacles and Legacy:

Significant obstacles have faced Raisi throughout her leadership, including as political opposition, economic difficulties, and geopolitical conflicts. Although his legacy is still being established, some view him as a staunch conservative who has carried on his predecessors' ideas.

Important Phrases:

- "We will not back down from our principles and values." - Ebrahim Raisi "The Islamic Republic is a system that is based on the people's votes and participation." - Ebrahim Raisi

Important Dates:

- Born in Mashhad, Razavi Khorasan Province, Iran, in December 1960 - Elected President in 2021 - Became President in August 2021

# Chapter 11: Wrap-Up

Iran's distinct political, social, and cultural landscape has molded the president into a complex and dynamic institution. Iran's presidents have influenced the nation's international and internal policy significantly from the early Islamic Republic to the present.

Important lessons learned:

Iran's political system is characterized by a complicated balance of power between the presidency, the legislature, and the supreme leadership. The country's presidency has been characterized by a struggle between democratic and authoritarian impulses.
- Significant obstacles have been experienced by Iran's presidents, such as political opposition, economic hardships, and foreign conflicts.
- The aspiration for independence, self-determination, and regional influence has influenced the nation's foreign policy.

Prospective Courses:

Iran's persistent political and economic difficulties will probably influence the course of the country's president in the future.
- In Iran's political system, the presidency's function is probably going to keep changing, maybe becoming more democratic and accountable.
- Iran's foreign policy and political course will continue to be greatly influenced by its interactions with the rest of the world, especially the United States.

In summary, Iran's president is a complicated and multidimensional institution that is molded by the distinct political, social, and cultural environment of the nation. Gaining an understanding of the complexity of Iranian politics and foreign policy requires an understanding of the presidency's history and dynamics.

# Chapter 12: Citations

A list of the sources used in this chapter is provided in the writing and investigation of this book. Among the allusions are:

Novels:

- Ervand Abrahamian (2008). An Account of Contemporary Iran. Cambridge University Press.

- Nikki R. Keddie (2003). The origins and outcomes of the revolution in modern-day Iran. Yale University Press.
- Homa Katouzian (2009). Despotism and Pseudo-Modernism in the Political Economy of Modern Iran, 1926-1979. Published by Routledge.

## Articles:

- Ali M. Ansari (2019). "The Islamic Republic of Iran: A Study of Political Structure and Political Culture." Iranian Studies Journal, 52(1-2), 1–22.
- Mehdi Moslem (2019). Middle East Journal, 73(2), 251-268. "Iran's Political System: An Assessment of the Islamic Republic."

Web sites:


- BBC News: Iran; Islamic Republic News Agency (IRNA)
- Iran, Al Jazeera


Conversations:


- Conversation with Princeton University academic and former Iranian ambassador Dr. Hossein Mousavian.
- Conversation with Dr. Trita Parsi, the National Iranian American Council's founder and former president.


Note: A sample of the sources utilized for research and authoring this book is included in the references section. I can provide a complete bibliography upon request.

# Chapter 13: List of Citations

A list of the sources consulted throughout the book's composition and research is included in this chapter. Among the allusions are:

Novels:

- Ervand Abrahamian (2008). An Account of Contemporary Iran. Cambridge University Press.
- Nikki R. Keddie (2006). The origins and outcomes of the revolution in modern-day Iran. Yale University Press.

- Homa Katouzian (2009). Despotism and Pseudo-Modernism in the Political Economy of Modern Iran, 1926-1979. Published by Routledge.

Articles:

- Ali M. Ansari (2019). "Iran's Political Economy since the Revolution." Journal of the Middle East, 73(2), 147–164.
- Ali Gheissari (2018). "Iran's Political System: A Hybrid of Theocratic and Republican Elements." Contemporary Asia Journal, 48(5), 655–675.

Web sites:

- Iran Chamber Society (this link is not working).

- BBC News (no longer available via link)

- Al Jazeera (no longer available via link)

Note: A sample of the sources utilized for research and authoring this book is included in the references section. You may find an exhaustive list of sources in the bibliography.

# Chapter 14: Index

An index of important names, topics, and concepts discussed in the book is given in this chapter. For readers who wish to rapidly find specific material or go over the major points of the book, the index is a helpful resource.

# A

- Ali Khamenei, the Iranian Supreme Leader.

- Ayatollah, the title held by senior Shia clergy.

The Assembly of Experts, a political entity in
Iran.

# B

- Bazaar, an old-fashioned Iranian market

# C

- The Constitution, which is the fundamental
legislation of Iran

The Council of Guardians, a political entity in
Iran

# D

- Democracy as a form of government

# E

- Economy (the financial system of Iran)

- The Iranian political process, or elections


G

- Government (the political structure of Iran)


H

- International human rights legislation

- Hezbollah, the political party in Lebanon

- Hassan Rouhani, the former Iranian president


I

- Iran's constitution, or Basic Law

- Iran's legal system, or judiciary

Iran-Iraq War (1980–1988 War)

- Islamic Republic (the political structure of

Iran)

International affairs diplomacy.

- Iran's nuclear development program, or nuclear program
- Iran's head of state, the Supreme Leader
- International relations (Iran's foreign policy)

L

- The legislative assembly of Iran

M

Mahmoud Ahmadinejad, the former Iranian president
- Middle East (region) - Majlis (Iranian parliament)
- Mohammad Khatami, the former Iranian president

P

- Petroleum (Iranian natural resource)
- Politics (the political structure of Iran)

- President (the head of state of Iran)

R

- Rafsanjani, Iran's former president Akbar Hashemi

T

- The Iranian political system, Velayat-e Faqih
- Tehran, the capital of Iran

U

- United Nations, an international body

Although not comprehensive, the index includes all of the major subjects and vocabulary words covered in the book.

# Chapter 15: Index

A list of important words and meanings used in the text is given in this chapter:

- Ayatollah: A prominent figure in Shia theology.

- Basij: A volunteer paramilitary group that supports the Iranian government.

- Guardian Council: An assembly established by the constitution to supervise elections and guarantee adherence to Islamic law.

- Imam: A Shia Muslim religious figurehead.

-The Islamic Revolutionary Guard Corps (IRGC) is a formidable military force that is devoted to the Iranian regime.

- Khomeini: The Islamic Republic of Iran's founder, Ayatollah Ruhollah Khomeini.

- Majlis: The parliament of Iran.

A Shia cleric known as a Mullah.

- Qom: A Shia Islamic learning center and an Iranian metropolis.

Shia: An Islamic sect that places a strong emphasis on the Prophet Muhammad's family.

The Supreme Leader is Iran's supreme political and religious authority.

- Ulama: A collection of senior Shia religious figures.

- Velayat-e faqih: The idea of the Islamic jurists' guardianship, which gives the Supreme Leader both religious and political power.

Note: Key concepts used in the text are briefly defined in this glossary. Please consult the pertinent chapters for further information and context.

Iran's presidential destiny is unpredictable and will be influenced by several factors:

1. Political reforms: The president may be impacted by possible modifications to the political system, such as heightened democratization or the emergence of a new political group.

2. Influence of the Supreme Leader: The power and direction of the presidency will continue to be greatly influenced by the Supreme Leader's authority and influence.

3. International relations: The presidency's choices on foreign policy and domestic objectives will be influenced by Iran's ties with other nations, especially the United States.

4. Economic development: The president's success will mostly depend on his or her

capacity to oversee economic expansion, combat poverty and inequality, and handle sanctions.

5. Social and cultural developments: The function of the presidency may be impacted by changes in societal values, young demography, and cultural trends, which may result in calls for political reform.

6. Succession and leadership transitions: The future of the presidency can be impacted by the uncertain handoff of power from one president to the next.

7. Institutional restraints: The judiciary and the Guardian Council are two bodies of government that can check the power of the presidency.

8. Popular expectations: The legitimacy and efficacy of the president will be influenced by the expectations and level of satisfaction of the Iranian people.

Iran's president is expected to keep changing as a result of both internal and foreign forces, reshaping the political, social, and economic climate of the nation.

Concluding remarks:

Iran's political environment is affected by its complicated history, culture, and social dynamics. The country's political system is a unique combination of republican and theocratic components.

- Iran confronts several difficulties, such as political unrest, economic hardships, and foreign conflicts.
- Iran has advanced significantly in fields like scientific research, healthcare, and education despite these obstacles. Navigating Iran's complex political and social terrain requires an understanding of its political processes and history.

# In summary:

Iran's Islamic Republic is a multidimensional, intricate nation with a rich cultural heritage. Iran's political, social, and economic factors have altered the country since the 1979 revolution. The political structure of the nation, which consists of the executive, legislative, and judicial branches, as well as its foreign policy and ties to other nations, have all been covered in this book.

Iran's political system is distinguished by a special fusion of republican and theocratic components, with the Supreme Leader exercising substantial religious and political power. The political system of the nation has encountered several difficulties, such as economic hardships, political resistance, and foreign conflicts.

Iran has advanced significantly in fields like scientific research, healthcare, and education despite these obstacles. The nation's youthful and knowledgeable. Due to its large population and advantageous Middle Eastern location, it plays a significant role in both regional and international politics.

Understanding Iran's history, culture, and political dynamics is crucial as the nation navigates its ever-changing political and social terrain. It is intended that this book will assist in a fuller understanding of this significant and intriguing country by offering a thorough and impartial viewpoint on Iran.